Traditional
FARMHOUSE TEAS

by Janice Murfitt
Illustrated by Julia Cobbold

First published in Great Britain in 1994 by
Parragon Book Service Ltd
Unit 13-17
Avonbridge Trading Estate
Atlantic Road
Avonmouth
Bristol BS11 9QD

ISBN 1 85813 683 0

Edited, designed and typeset by Haldane Mason
Editor: Joanna Swinnerton

Printed in Italy

Note: Cup measurements in this book are for American cups. Tablespoons are assumed to be 15ml. Unless otherwise stated, milk is assumed to be full-fat, eggs are standard size 2 and pepper is freshly ground black pepper.

CONTENTS

SANDWICHES

Sandwiches were invented by the 4th Earl of Sandwich, who was a very keen card player, and would become so absorbed in the game that he would order pieces of meat to be placed between slices of bread so that he could eat and play the game at the same time.

MAKES 16

8 large slices white or brown bread

butter for spreading

FILLINGS

1 hard-boiled (hard-cooked) egg, chopped

1 tbsp mustard and cress

1 tbsp mayonnaise

2 tbsp flaked red salmon

1 tsp malt vinegar

6 slices peeled cucumber

2 tbsp grated cheese

2 tsp finely chopped spring onions (scallions)

½ tsp wholegrain mustard

1 large slice prime-quality ham

salt and pepper

1 Spread each slice of bread evenly with butter.

2 Combine the chopped egg with the mustard and cress, mayonnaise and some salt and pepper until well blended. Spread over a slice of bread.

3 Mix the flaked salmon with the vinegar and some salt and pepper. Spread over a slice of bread and top with cucumber slices.

4 Spread the grated cheese, spring onions (scallions) and some salt and pepper over another slice of bread.

5 Spread the mustard over a slice of bread and top with a slice of ham. Sprinkle over a little pepper.

6 Place the remaining bread slices on top of the fillings, press down gently, cut off the crusts if you prefer and cut into quarters.

7 Cover with clingfilm (plastic wrap) to prevent drying, or serve immediately.

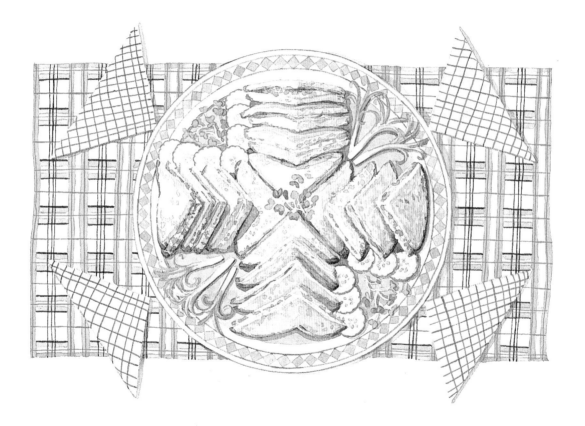

POTATO CAKES

These potato cakes are an excellent way of using up leftover potato, and make a substantial teatime snack. You can use other fruits, such as pears, plums or apricots, in place of the apple.

MAKES 12

500 g/1 lb/2 cups cooked mashed potato

30 g/1 oz/2 tbsp butter, melted

1 tsp caster (superfine) sugar

1 tsp ground ginger

125 g/4 oz/1 cup plain (all-purpose) flour

1 dessert apple, grated

TO SERVE

butter

caster (superfine) sugar

1 Put the potato into a large mixing bowl and add the butter, sugar and ginger. Mix together with a wooden spoon until well blended.

2 Add the flour and mix to form a firm dough. Roll out to a thickness of 5 mm/ ¼ inch. Using a 6 cm/2½ inch plain cutter, cut out 24 rounds, re-rolling as necessary.

3 Divide the grated apple between 12 of the rounds. Moisten the edges with water. Place the remaining rounds over the filling and pinch the edges together to seal.

4 Heat a griddle or frying pan (skillet) and grease lightly. Arrange a few cakes on the griddle or pan (skillet) and cook for 3–4 minutes until golden brown.

5 Turn over each cake and cook the other side until golden brown.

6 Make a hole in the top of each potato cake, insert a thin slice of butter and dredge thickly with sugar. Serve immediately.

ANCHOVY TOAST

Anchovy essence (paste) is sometimes also known as Gentleman's Relish. It is an acquired taste, as it is deliciously strong and salty.

SERVES 4

30 g/1 oz/2 tbsp butter

2 tbsp anchovy essence (paste)

2 tsp plain (all-purpose) flour

1 tbsp water

4 slices bread

2 hard-boiled (hard-cooked) eggs, halved

1 Melt the butter in a small saucepan, stir in the anchovy essence (paste) and add the flour.

2 Remove the saucepan from the heat, add the water and beat until smooth. Return to the heat and cook for 1 minute.

3 Toast the slices of bread on one side. Spread the anchovy mixture on the untoasted side.

4 Place the toast under a preheated hot grill (broiler) until golden brown. Cut into triangles and serve each slice with half a hard-boiled (hard-cooked) egg.

CINNAMON TOAST

This is a simple and popular tea-time snack that smells delicious as the butter, sugar and cinnamon melt together under the grill.

1 Toast the slices of bread on one side only until golden brown.

2 Mix together the cinnamon and caster (superfine) sugar until well blended.

3 Spread the untoasted side of each slice of bread with butter and sprinkle generously with the cinnamon and sugar mixture.

4 Place under a preheated moderate grill (broiler) and cook slowly until the toast is golden brown. Cut into fingers to serve.

10

DROP SCONES WITH HERB BUTTER

MAKES 20

175 g/6 oz/1¼ cups plain (all-purpose) flour

¼ tsp salt

1½ tsp baking powder

60 g/2 oz/⅓ cup medium oatmeal

15 g/½ oz/1 tbsp butter

1 egg, beaten

300 ml/½ pint/1¼ cups milk

HERB BUTTER

125 g/4 oz/½ cup slightly salted butter

2 tsp each of chopped fresh rosemary, sage and oregano

These are also known as griddle cakes, as they were first cooked by dropping batter in spoonfuls on to a hot griddle over an open fire.

1 Sift the flour, salt and baking powder into a mixing bowl. Add the oatmeal.

2 Rub in the butter until the mixture resembles fine breadcrumbs. Stir in the egg and half of the milk. Mix together with a wooden spoon until evenly mixed.

3 Stir in the remaining milk and beat until smooth. Cover with clingfilm (plastic wrap) and leave in a cool place for 30 minutes.

4 To make the herb butter, beat the butter well with a wooden spoon until soft. Stir in the herbs.

5 Heat a griddle or large frying pan (skillet) and brush lightly with oil. Drop 4 medium-sized spoonfuls of mixture on the hot surface.

6 Cook until each scone looks set on the top. Using a palette knife, turn each scone and

cook for a further 1–2 minutes until golden brown.

7 Place the scones on a plate covered with a clean linen napkin and keep them warm while cooking the remaining batter. Serve the scones warm, spread with herb butter.

RICH CHOCOLATE CAKE

A good, rich chocolate cake is an essential part of any afternoon tea. Everyone has their favourite recipe, but this luxurious version should please most tastes.

SERVES 10

2 tbsp cocoa powder

2 tbsp boiling water

175 g/6 oz/¾ cup unsalted butter

175 g/6 oz/¾ cup caster (superfine) sugar

3 eggs

175 g/6 oz/1½ cups self-raising flour

60 g/2 oz/½ cup ground almonds

icing (confectioners') sugar, for dusting

ICING (FROSTING)

125 g/4 oz/4 squares plain (dark) chocolate

60 g/2 oz/¼ cup unsalted butter

1 egg

175 g/6 oz/1⅓ cups icing (confectioners') sugar, sifted

60 g/2 oz/2 squares white chocolate

1 Grease and line the base of 2 x 20 cm/8 inch sandwich tins (layer pans) with greaseproof paper (baking parchment).

2 Blend the cocoa powder and boiling water together.

3 Beat the butter and sugar together until light and fluffy. Add the eggs one at a time, beating after each addition. Beat in the cocoa mixture.

4 Sift the flour into the bowl, add the ground almonds and fold in until all the flour has been incorporated.

5 Divide the mixture equally between the cake tins (pans) and smooth the tops. Bake in a preheated oven at 170°C, 325°F, Gas Mark 3 for 30–35 minutes or until the cakes spring back when pressed in the centre. Loosen edges with a palette knife and turn the cakes out. Remove the paper (parchment) and cool on a wire rack.

6 To make the icing (frosting), melt the chocolate and butter in a bowl over gently simmering water, stirring occasionally. Remove from the heat and beat in the egg. Stir in the icing (confectioners') sugar and beat until smooth and glossy.

7 Sandwich the cakes together with a quarter of the icing (frosting) and pour the rest of it over the cake. Spread evenly to coat

the top and sides. Using a potato peeler, shave the white chocolate into curls. Pile these on top of the cake and dust with icing (confectioners') sugar. Leave in a cool place to set.

LEMON SWISS (JELLY) ROLL

Lemon balm was once grown prolifically in cottage gardens and was often strewn over the wooden floors, as it gave a sweet refreshing perfume when trodden on. If unavailable, use lemon geranium leaves, or add the grated rind of 1 lemon to the cake mixture.

SERVES 8

8 fresh lemon balm leaves

4 eggs, separated

1 tbsp orange flower water or 1 tbsp lemon juice

1 tbsp cold water

185 g/6½ oz/¾ cup plus 1 tbsp caster (superfine) sugar

90 g/3 oz/¾ cup plain (all-purpose) flour

15 g/½ oz/2 tbsp cornflour (cornstarch)

4 tbsp lemon curd

caster (superfine) sugar for dusting

1 Lightly grease and line a 33 x 23 cm/13 x 9 inch Swiss (jelly) roll tin (pan) with greaseproof paper (baking parchment). Arrange the lemon balm leaves over the base of the tin (pan).

2 Whisk the egg yolks well, then add the orange flower water (or lemon juice) and cold water gradually until well blended. Add 150 g/5 oz/⅔ cup of the caster (superfine) sugar and whisk until thick and pale.

3 Using clean beaters, whisk the egg whites until stiff, then whisk in the remaining sugar until stiff. Using a plastic-bladed spatula, fold the egg whites into the yolks until all the egg white has been incorporated.

4 Sift the flour and cornflour (cornstarch) over the surface and fold into the mixture. Pour the mixture into the prepared tin (pan) and shake gently to level the surface.

5 Place in a preheated oven at 180°C, 350°, Gas Mark 4 and bake for 12–15 minutes until lightly browned and well risen,

or until the cake springs back when pressed in the centre.

6 Turn the sponge out on to a lightly sugared piece of greaseproof paper (baking parchment). Remove the leaves, trim off the edges and spread the sponge with lemon curd. Roll up from the short edge into a neat roll and leave to cool on a wire rack with the join underneath. Dust with caster (superfine) sugar.

COFFEE AND WALNUT CAKE

The essential bitterness of coffee makes it a perfect complement to sweet flavours. In this classic cake, the distinctive taste of the walnuts enhances the aromatic coffee flavour.

SERVES 10

125 g/4 oz/1 cup walnut halves

175 g/6 oz/¾ cup unsalted butter, softened

175 g/6 oz/¾ cup caster (superfine) sugar

3 eggs

200 g/7 oz/1¾ cups self-raising flour, sifted

COFFEE BUTTER ICING
(FROSTING)

4 tsp instant coffee granules dissolved in 2 tbsp boiling water, then left to cool

500 g/1 lb/3½ cups icing (confectioners') sugar, sifted

250 g/8 oz/1 cup unsalted butter, softened

1 Lightly grease and line the base of 2 x 20 cm /8 inch round sandwich tins (layer pans) with greaseproof paper (baking parchment).

2 Chop 60 g/2 oz/½ cup of the walnuts finely and keep the remaining halves for decoration.

3 Put the butter and sugar into a bowl and beat with a wooden spoon for 2–3 minutes until light and fluffy. Add the eggs one at a time, beating well between each egg, until the mixture is thick and smooth.

4 Sift the flour into the creamed mixture, add the chopped walnuts and fold in with a plastic-bladed spatula until evenly blended.

5 Divide the mixture between the tins (pans) and bake in a preheated oven at 170°C, 325°F, Gas Mark 3 for 30–40 minutes or until the cakes spring back when pressed in the centre.

6 Loosen the edges with a palette knife and turn the cakes out. Remove the paper (parchment) and leave to cool on a wire rack. When cool, cut each cake in half to make 4 layers.

7 To make the icing (frosting), blend the cooled coffee, icing (confectioners') sugar and butter and beat with a wooden spoon until light and fluffy.

8 Sandwich the layers together with one third of the icing (frosting). Put 4 tbsp of it into a piping bag with a small star nozzle (tip). Spread the remainder evenly over the top and sides of the cake and smooth the surface with a palette knife dipped in hot water. Pipe a border of icing (frosting) around the top and base of the cake and decorate with the reserved walnut halves.

CURD CAKE

The slightly tart taste and the firm texture of the creamy curd cheese make this a delicious and satisfying dessert.

SERVES 8

semolina for dusting

90 g/3 oz/⅓ cup unsalted butter, softened

175 g/6 oz/¾ cup caster (superfine) sugar

500 g/1 lb/2 cups curd (low-fat soft) cheese

3 eggs, separated

90 g/3 oz/¾ cup ground almonds

1 tsp mixed spice (apple pie spice)

grated rind of 1 lemon

4 tbsp lemon juice

90 g/3 oz/½ cup semolina

90 g/3 oz/½ cup currants

icing (confectioners') sugar for dusting

1 Lightly grease a 23 cm/9 inch springform tin (pan) and line the base with greaseproof paper (baking parchment). Dust with semolina.

2 Beat the butter and sugar together with a wooden spoon until light and fluffy.

3 Add the curd (low-fat soft) cheese and beat until well blended. Stir in the egg yolks and beat until smooth. Beat in the almonds, spice, lemon rind and juice, semolina and currants until well blended.

4 Whisk the egg whites in a clean bowl until stiff. Fold into the cheese mixture until all the egg whites have been incorporated. Pour the mixture into the prepared tin (pan).

5 Place in a preheated oven at 150°C, 300°F, Gas Mark 2 and bake for 1–1¼ hours or until the mixture has set and springs back when pressed in the centre. Leave to cool in the tin (pan).

6 Turn out the cake, remove the paper (parchment) carefully and place the cake on a serving plate. Dust lightly with the icing (confectioners') sugar.

CARAWAY SEED CAKE

Seed cakes were once baked to celebrate the coming harvest. Caraway seeds growing wild were threshed in the fields in a cloth, and were widely used by pastry cooks. They are believed to be good for the digestion.

SERVES 8

250 g/8 oz/1 cup butter, softened

250 g/8 oz/1 cup caster (superfine) sugar

5 eggs, separated

250 g/8 oz/2 cups plain (all-purpose) flour

¼ tsp grated nutmeg

¼ tsp ground cloves

2 tsp caraway seeds

2 tbsp ale (beer), dry white wine or brandy

6 sugar lumps, crushed

extra caraway seeds for sprinkling

1 Lightly grease and line the base and sides of a 20 cm/ 8 inch round cake tin (pan) with greaseproof paper (baking parchment).

2 Beat the butter in a mixing bowl with a wooden spoon until soft. Add the sugar and beat until light and fluffy.

3 Add the egg yolks, one at a time, each with 1 tbsp of the flour, beating well after each addition. Sift the rest of the flour, the nutmeg and cloves into the bowl and add the caraway seeds.

4 Whisk the egg whites in a clean bowl until stiff and add half of them to the cake mixture. Using a plastic-bladed spatula, fold the egg whites into the mixture until all the flour has been incorporated. Fold in the remaining egg white and ale (beer), wine or brandy.

5 Place the cake mixture into the tin (pan) and level the top. Sprinkle with the crushed sugar and a few caraway seeds.

6 Place in a pre-heated oven at 170°C, 325°F, Gas Mark 3 and bake for about 55–60 minutes until well risen and golden brown, or until the cake springs back when

pressed in the centre. Leave to cool in the tin (pan) for 10 minutes before turning out. Remove the paper and cool the cake on a wire rack. To serve, either cut into wedges or cut large slices across the cake.

APPLE CAKE

Apples have almost endless uses in the kitchen, as different varieties are grown for cooking, eating and cider-making. The sharpness of cooking apples give a bite to this cake, which is served with clotted cream.

SERVES 8

250 g/8 oz/2 cups self-raising flour

½ tsp ground cloves

1 tsp ground cinnamon

125 g/4 oz/½ cup butter

175 g/6 oz/¾ cup caster (superfine) sugar

500 g/1 lb cooking apples

2 eggs, beaten

granulated sugar for sprinkling

clotted or whipped cream

1 Lightly grease and line the base and side of a 20 cm/8 inch round cake tin (pan) with greaseproof paper (baking parchment).

2 Sift the flour, cloves and cinnamon into a mixing bowl. Cut the butter into small pieces and rub into the flour with your fingertips until the mixture resembles fine breadcrumbs.

3 Stir in the caster (superfine) sugar. Peel, core and chop the apples and add to the mixture with the beaten eggs. Mix together with a wooden spoon and beat until soft and smooth.

4 Turn the mixture into the cake tin (pan) and smooth the top. Place in a preheated oven at 170°C, 325°F, Gas Mark 3 and bake for 1–1¼ hours until the cake is well risen and springs back when pressed in the centre.

5 Leave to cool in the tin (pan) for 5 minutes. Turn out, remove the paper (parchment)

and place the cake on a wire rack. Sprinkle the top with granulated sugar.

6 This cake is best eaten fresh. Serve it warm with a bowl of clotted cream.

PORTER CAKE

SERVES 8

125 g/4 oz/½ cup butter

4 tbsp golden (light corn) syrup

2 tbsp treacle (molasses)

180 ml/6 fl oz/¾ cup stout

250 g/8 oz/1⅓ cups raisins

250 g/8 oz/1⅓ cups currants

125 g/4 oz/⅔ cup sultanas
(golden raisins)

125 g/4 oz/⅔ cup each of stoned
(pitted) dates and stoned (pitted)
prunes, chopped

125 g/4 oz/⅔ cup cut mixed peel

250 g/8 oz/2 cups plain (all-
purpose) flour

1 tsp each grated nutmeg and
allspice

2 eggs, beaten

½ tsp bicarbonate of soda
(baking soda)

*Porter was once considered to be very strengthening
because of its nutritional value – it certainly makes a
very rich, moist, dark fruit cake.*

1 Put the butter, syrup, treacle (molasses) and stout in a large saucepan. Heat gently, stirring occasionally until the butter has melted.

2 Bring to the boil and add the raisins, currants, sultanas (golden raisins), dates, prunes and peel. Stir to blend well, bring back to the boil and simmer very gently for 5 minutes. Remove from the heat and leave until lukewarm.

3 Grease and line the base and sides of a 20 cm/8 inch round cake tin (pan) with greaseproof paper (baking parchment). Tie a double-thick band of brown paper around the outside of the tin (pan) and stand on a baking sheet lined with a double-thickness of paper.

4 Sift the flour, nutmeg and allspice into a mixing bowl and add the beaten eggs.

5 Stir the bicarbonate of soda (baking soda) into the fruit mixture until well blended. Pour the fruit mixture into the flour and eggs and mix together with a wooden spoon.

6 Beat until thoroughly mixed, then put into the prepared tin (pan) and smooth the top. Place in a preheated oven at 150°C, 300°F, Gas Mark 2 and bake for 1¼–1½ hours.

7 When a warmed skewer inserted into the centre of the cake comes out clean, the cake is cooked. Leave to cool in the tin (pan), then turn out, remove the lining paper (parchment) and wrap in fresh greaseproof paper (baking parchment) or foil to keep moist. Store in an airtight tin.

SIMNEL CAKE

Simnel cake is one of the world's oldest festival cakes. The eleven decorative balls represent the Apostles – excluding Judas, the traitor.

SERVES 8

350 g/12 oz/2 cups mixed dried fruit

grated rind and juice of 1 small orange

175 g/6 oz/¾ cup butter, softened

175 g/6 oz/1 cup light soft brown sugar

250 g/8 oz/2 cups self-raising flour

3 eggs

2 tbsp apricot jam (preserves), boiled and sieved (strained)

350 g/12 oz yellow marzipan (almond paste)

TOPPING

2 tbsp sifted icing (confectioners') sugar

2 tsp orange juice

crystallized violets and rose petals

1 Grease and line an 18 cm/ 7 inch round cake tin (pan) with greaseproof paper (baking parchment). Tie a double-thick band of brown paper around the outside of the tin (pan) and place it on a baking sheet lined with a double thickness of paper.

2 Combine the dried fruit, orange rind and juice. Beat the butter together with the sugar, flour and eggs for 1–2 minutes until smooth and glossy. Add the dried fruit mixture and stir to combine evenly. Place half the mixture in the tin (pan) and smooth the top.

3 Roll out half the marzipan (almond paste) and trim to an 18 cm/7 inch round. Place

this on top of the mixture in the tin (pan) and smooth the rest of the cake mixture over the top.

4 Bake in a preheated oven at 150°C, 300°F, Gas Mark 2 for 2½–2¾ hours, or until a skewer inserted into the centre of the cake comes out clean. Leave to cool in the tin (pan) before turning out. Remove the paper and cool on a wire rack.

5 Brush the jam (preserves) over the top of the cake. Roll out three quarters of the remaining marzipan and trim to an 18 cm/7 inch round. Place on top of the cake and flute the edge with your fingertips. Shape the remaining marzipan into 11 balls and arrange on the top of

the cake. Place the cake under a preheated hot grill (broiler) until the top is evenly browned. Leave until cold.

6 Mix enough orange juice with the icing (confectioners') sugar to form the consistency of thick cream, and spread over the centre of the cake. When this has set, decorate the cake with rose petals and crystallized violets.

SALLY LUNN

Some say that this pale yellow bun with a golden glazed top is named after the woman who first made and sold them; others say that it is a derivation of the French cake 'Sol et Luneîi' ('Sun and Moon') as it took from sunrise to sunset to make.

SERVES 4

20 g/¾ oz/¾ cake fresh yeast or 1 sachet (envelope) easy-blend yeast

200 ml/7 fl oz/scant cup warm milk

350 g/12 oz/3 cups strong (bread) plain white flour

1 tsp salt

2 tsp mixed spice (apple pie spice)

45 g/1½ oz/3 tbsp caster (superfine) sugar

1 egg, beaten

60 g/2 oz/¼ cup butter, melted

TO GLAZE

1 egg yolk, beaten

4 sugar lumps, crushed

1 Blend the yeast and milk together in a warmed bowl. Sift 125 g/4 oz/1 cup of the flour over the surface, cover with clingfilm (plastic wrap) and leave to rise in a warm place for 30 minutes.

2 Grease an 18 cm/7 inch round cake tin (pan) or 4 x 6 cm/4 inch bun tins (pans). Line the bases with greaseproof paper (baking parchment).

3 Sift the remaining flour, salt and spice into the bowl, and add the sugar, egg and butter. Using a wooden spoon, stir to combine, then beat to a smooth batter.

4 Pour into the prepared cake tin (pan), cover with clingfilm (plastic wrap) and leave in a warm place until doubled in size.

5 Brush the top of the dough with the egg yolk and sprinkle with the crushed sugar. Bake in a preheated oven at 200°C, 400°F, Gas Mark 6 for 35–40 minutes until well risen and golden brown.

6 Cover the surface with greaseproof paper (baking

parchment) if it becomes too brown. Remove from the tin (pan) and cool on a wire rack.

7 Serve split and filled with whipped cream or spread thickly with butter.

LARDY CAKE

The yeast dough that makes this delicious cake is crammed full of lard, fruit and spices. When baked it should never be cut, only broken across the lines, and should be eaten on the same day it is made.

SERVES 8

DOUGH

1 sachet easy-blend dried yeast

1 tsp caster (superfine) sugar

150 ml/¼ pint/⅔ cup warm water

250 g/8 oz/2 cups strong plain white (bread) flour

1 tsp salt

15 g/½ oz/1 tbsp lard

FILLING

175 g/6 oz/¾ cup lard

125 g/4 oz/½ cup granulated sugar

250 g/8 oz/1⅓ cups mixed dried fruit

½ tsp mixed spice (apple pie spice)

1 tbsp clear honey

1 Combine the yeast, sugar and water in a bowl. Cover and leave until frothy, about 10 minutes.

2 Sift the flour and salt into a bowl and rub in the lard with your fingertips until it resembles fine breadcrumbs. Mix in the yeast liquid, knead into a dough, then knead until pliable and soft, (about 10 minutes) or work in a food processor for 3 minutes.

3 Cover the dough with cling-film (plastic wrap) and leave in a warm place until doubled in size. Roll out to a rectangle 30 x 20 cm/12 x 8 inches.

4 For the filling, arrange small pieces of lard over the top two thirds of the dough. Mix together the sugar, fruit and spice. Sprinkle half the mixture over the dough. Fold the bottom third of the dough up to the centre and the top third down. Seal the edges together well. Give the dough a quarter turn to the left and roll into a rectangle. Repeat the process using the remaining lard and fruit mixture. Turn the dough to the left again and repeat the rolling, folding and turning once more.

5 Roll out the dough to fit the base of a 25 x 20 cm/10 x 8 inch roasting tin (pan) brushed with melted lard, and cover with clingfilm (plastic wrap). Leave in a warm place until doubled in size. Score across the top with a sharp knife. Bake in a preheated oven at 200°C, 400°F, Gas Mark 6 for 25–30 minutes, basting with the sugary liquid that the cake produces. Brush the surface with honey 5 minutes before the end of the cooking time and leave the cake to cool in the tin to absorb the liquid before placing on a wire rack to cool.

MUFFINS

Muffins are a comforting tea-time treat, and seem to have been specially made for eating by the fire on a cold winter afternoon. Muffins should be split around the edges and toasted on both sides, then pulled apart to be buttered.

MAKES 12

300 ml/½ pint/1¼ cups milk

1 sachet easy-blend dried yeast

1 tsp caster (superfine) sugar

500 g/1 lb/4 cups strong plain white (bread) flour

2 tsp salt

1 tsp semolina

1 Warm the milk, add the yeast and sugar and blend well. Cover with clingfilm (plastic wrap), and leave for 10 minutes until frothy.

2 Sift the flour and salt into a warmed mixing bowl. Add the yeast liquid and mix to form a soft dough. Turn out on to a lightly floured work surface (counter) and knead for about 10 minutes until smooth and pliable. Return the dough to the bowl, cover with clingfilm (plastic wrap) and leave in a warm place until doubled in size.

3 Knead the dough until smooth, then roll out to a thickness of 1 cm/½ inch and cut into 12 rounds using a 7.5 cm/3 inch plain cutter.

4 Place the rounds well spaced on a floured baking sheet. Dust with semolina, cover with clingfilm (plastic wrap) and leave to rise until doubled in size.

5 Lightly grease a griddle or large frying pan (skillet) and place over a moderate heat. Place 2 or 3 muffins a little apart on the griddle and cook for 3 minutes until golden brown. Turn the muffins over, press

down with a palette knife and cook for a further 3–4 minutes until golden brown. Leave to cool on a wire rack while you cook the remaining muffins.

6 Slit around the outside of each muffin with a sharp knife. Toast on both sides, then split apart and spread with butter. Serve immediately.

CHELSEA BUNS

Spirals of sweet dough are filled with fruit and crushed sugar, and coated with golden (light corn) syrup before cooling to make a toothsome treat.

MAKES 12

120 ml/4 fl oz//½ cup milk

1 sachet easy-blend dried yeast

250 g/8 oz/2 cups strong plain white (bread) flour

½ tsp salt

60 g/2 oz/¼ cup butter

1 egg, beaten

125 g/4 oz/⅔ cup mixed dried fruit

60 g/2 oz/⅓ cup soft light brown sugar

1 tbsp golden (light corn) syrup

1 Lightly butter an 18 cm/ 7 inch square tin. Blend together the milk and yeast in a bowl, cover with clingfilm (plastic wrap) and leave until frothy.

2 Sift the flour and salt into a large, warmed mixing bowl, add half the butter and rub into the flour with your fingertips until the mixture resembles fine breadcrumbs.

3 Add the yeast liquid and beaten egg and mix together to form a dough. Knead lightly until smooth.

4 Turn out on to a lightly floured work surface (counter) and knead for about 10 minutes until smooth and

pliable. Alternatively, work in a food processor for 3 minutes. Return the dough to the bowl, cover with clingfilm (plastic wrap) and leave in a warm place until doubled in size.

5 Knead the dough lightly until smooth and roll out to a rectangle about 30 x 23 cm/12 x 9 inches.

6 Mix together the dried fruit and sugar. Melt the remaining butter and brush the surface of the dough. Cover with the dried fruit mixture. Roll up the dough from the long edge into a neat roll, pressing the edges together to seal well. Cut the roll into 12 pieces and arrange in the tin (pan), cut side

uppermost. Cover with clingfilm (plastic wrap) and leave until doubled in size.

7 Brush the tops of the buns with any remaining butter. Place in a preheated oven at 190°C, 375°F, Gas Mark 5. Bake for about 30 minutes until well risen and golden brown. Brush with warmed golden (light corn) syrup and leave to cool in the tin (pan) for 5 minutes before turning out and cooling on a wire rack.

CREAM SCONES

Scones were first cooked on a griddle, but when they were later baked in ovens, it resulted in a lighter, more risen scone. A traditional afternoon tea should always include freshly baked scones split and filled with jam and clotted cream.

MAKES 12

250 g/8 oz/2 cups self-raising flour

1 tsp baking powder

¼ tsp salt

30 g/1 oz/2 tbsp caster (superfine) sugar

60 g/2 oz/¼ cup butter

120 ml/4 fl oz/½ cup milk

FILLING

4 tbsp strawberry jam (preserves)

150 ml/¼ pint/⅔ cup clotted or whipped cream

1 Lightly flour 2 baking sheets.

2 Sift the flour, baking powder and salt into a mixing bowl. Add the sugar. Cut the butter into pieces, and rub into the flour with your fingertips until the mixture resembles fine breadcrumbs.

3 Stir in the milk, using a fork, and mix to a soft dough. Turn out on to a floured work surface (counter) and knead lightly.

4 Roll out the dough to a thickness of 1 cm/½ inch and cut out 12 rounds using a 5 cm/2 inch plain cutter, re-kneading and re-rolling as necessary.

5 Arrange well spaced on the baking sheets. Bake in a preheated oven at 220°C, 425°F, Gas Mark 7 for 12–15 minutes or until well risen and pale golden. Leave to cool on a wire rack.

6 To serve, split the scones in half and spread with jam (preserves) and clotted or whipped cream.

WALNUT CHEESE LOAF

Walnuts can be used for pickling when green, as well as for cooking or eating fresh when ripe. Teamed with Cheddar cheese, this makes a tasty teabread.

SERVES 10

350 g/12 oz/3 cups self-raising flour

1½ tsp baking powder

1 tsp mustard powder

1 tsp salt

pepper

125 g/4 oz/½ cup butter

175 g/6 oz/1½ cups Cheddar cheese, grated

125 g/4 oz/1 cup walnuts, chopped

1 tbsp chopped fresh chives

1 tbsp chopped parsley

2 eggs

150 ml/¼ pint/⅔ cup milk

1 Line the base and sides of a 1 kg/2 lb loaf tin (pan) with greaseproof paper.

2 Sift the flour, baking powder, mustard, salt and pepper into a mixing bowl. Cut the butter into small pieces and rub into the flour with your fingertips until the mixture resembles fine breadcrumbs.

3 Stir in the cheese, walnuts, chives, parsley, eggs and milk. Mix together with a wooden spoon and beat for 1–2 minutes until well blended.

4 Place the mixture in the prepared tin (pan) and spread out to level the top. Bake in a preheated oven at 190°C, 375°F, Gas Mark 5 for about 1 hour until the mixture is well risen, golden brown and a skewer inserted into the centre comes out clean.

5 Leave to cool in the tin (pan) for 5 minutes before turning out. Remove the greaseproof paper (baking parchment) and leave to cool on a wire rack. Serve warm or cold, cut into slices.

GRIDDLED FRUIT SCONE

Affectionately known as a 'Singing Hinny', this large round cake made of scone mixture is baked on a griddle, where it sings and fizzes while it cooks.

SERVES 6

250 g/8 oz/2 cups plain (all-purpose) flour

¼ tsp bicarbonate of soda (baking soda)

½ tsp cream of tartar

½ tsp salt

90 g/3 oz/⅓ cup lard

125 g/4 oz/⅔ cup currants

120 ml/4 fl oz/½ cup milk

1 Sift the flour, bicarbonate of soda (baking soda), cream of tartar and salt into a mixing bowl.

2 Cut the lard into pieces and rub into the flour with your fingertips until the mixture resembles fine breadcrumbs. Stir in the currants and, using a fork, stir in enough milk to form a soft dough.

3 Heat the griddle or a large frying pan (skillet) over a moderate heat for 2–3 minutes.

4 Knead the dough on a lightly floured work surface until smooth. Roll out to a 20 cm/8 inch round.

5 Grease the griddle or frying pan (skillet) lightly, place the round of dough in the centre and cook the underside slowly for about 10 minutes.

6 Using a fish slice, turn the round over and cook for a further 10 minutes. Remove the scone from the griddle and split in half using a sharp knife. Spread with butter and sandwich together. Cut into wedges and serve hot.

TEA BRACK

This moist fruit bread is made by steeping the dried fruit in tea overnight. This originates from a time when herbal tea infusions were common, and leftover tea was used for tea breads.

SERVES 12

300 ml/½ pint/1¼ cups warm herbal tea

500 g/1 lb/3 cups mixed dried fruit

250 g/8 oz/1⅓ cups light soft brown sugar

3 tbsp orange marmalade

1 egg, beaten

500g/1 lb/4 cups self-raising flour

1 tsp ground allspice

1 Put the tea, mixed dried fruit, sugar and marmalade into a large mixing bowl. Stir until well blended, cover and leave to soak overnight.

2 Grease 2 x 500 g/1 lb or 1 x 1 kg/2 lb loaf tins (pans). Line the base and sides with greaseproof paper (baking parchment).

3 Add the egg to the fruit mixture and sift in the flour and allspice. Mix together with a wooden spoon and beat until blended.

4 Place the mixture in the large tin (pan) or divide between the two smaller tins (pans). Level the tops.

5 Place in a preheated oven at 170°C, 325°F, Gas Mark 3 and bake for about 1¼ hours until well risen. Test by pressing with your fingers; if cooked, the fruit bread should spring back and feel firm.

6 Leave to cool in the tin (pan) for 5 minutes before turning out. Remove the paper and leave to cool on a wire rack.

7 Serve cut into slices and buttered generously. This bread will keep moist if wrapped in foil, and improves with keeping.

OATCAKES

This recipe dates back to the twelfth century, and was once known as 'haver bread'. Haver bread was baked on a bake stone at the side of the fireplace, and hung on a rack suspended from the ceiling.

MAKES 12

450 ml/¾ pint/scant 2 cups warm water

1 tsp easy-blend dried yeast

175 g/6 oz/1 cup fine oatmeal

½ tsp salt

oatmeal for sprinkling

1 Blend the water and yeast together in a bowl. Add the oatmeal and salt and mix together with a wooden spoon until thoroughly blended.

2 Cover the bowl with a cloth and leave in a warm place until well risen, about 1 hour.

3 Heat a griddle, stir the oatmeal mixture and thin with some warm water if necessary. Sprinkle the griddle with a little extra oatmeal in a long strip about 5 cm/2 inches wide.

4 Pour a thin line of the oatmeal mixture over the strip and spread out very thinly into an oblong.

5 Cook for less than a minute, remove from the heat and cut into 3 pieces. Turn over with a palette knife, then place over a rolling pin covered with a clean cloth to cool.

6 Repeat to make more oatcakes until all the mixture has been used.

GINGERBREAD

This originated in the village of Grasmere in northern England, and is made from oatmeal, spices and syrup. The shop still exists where the gingerbread has been made to a secret recipe since 1855.

1 Lightly grease a 20 cm/8 inch round cake tin (pan) at least 5 cm/2 inches deep, and line the base with greaseproof paper (baking parchment).

2 Put the oatmeal, flour, bicarbonate of soda (baking soda), cream of tartar, ginger and brown sugar into a large mixing bowl.

3 Cut the butter into pieces and rub into the flour mixture with your fingertips until it resembles fine breadcrumbs.

4 Drizzle in the golden (light corn) syrup and mix with a fork until the mixture begins to bind together.

5 Press into the tin (pan) until level.

Place in a preheated oven at 170°C, 325°F, Gas Mark 3 and bake for 30–35 minutes until golden brown. Sprinkle with the crushed sugar and leave to cool in the tin (pan).

SWEET PASTRY PUFFS

MAKES 12

500 g/1 lb ready-made (store-bought) puff pastry

250 g/8 oz/³/₄ cup mincemeat or jam (preserves)

granulated sugar for sprinkling

These are also known as Coventry God Cakes, and were a good luck cake given by godparents to their godchildren. Made as triangles to represent the church spires in the city, they were filled with mincemeat or jam.

1 Cut the pastry in half, roll out 1 piece and trim to a rectangle 30 x 20 cm/12 x 8 inches. Cut in half and then into 6 squares, each measuring 10 cm/4 inches. Repeat with the remaining pastry.

2 Moisten the edges of each square with water and place a spoonful of mincemeat or jam (preserves) in the centre. Fold each square into a triangle, seal the edges well and brush the top of each triangle with a little water.

3 Spread some sugar on to a plate and invert each triangle on to it to coat the top. Make three slits across the top with a sharp knife. Place the pastry triangles on a floured baking sheet.

4 Place in a preheated oven at 220°C, 425°F, Gas Mark 7 and bake for 15–20 minutes until well-risen and golden brown. Leave to cool on a wire rack.

MACAROONS

These little cakes originated from a time when almonds were more commonly used in the kitchen than they are now. Ground finely and blended with rosewater, violets and sugar, they were served as a sweetmeat.

MAKES 20

125 g/4 oz/1 cup ground almonds

125 g/4 oz/½ cup caster (superfine) sugar

½ tsp almond flavouring (extract)

2 egg whites, whisked

10 blanched almonds, split

icing (confectioners') sugar for dusting

1 Line 2 baking sheets with rice paper.

2 Put the ground almonds, sugar and almond flavouring (extract) into a bowl. Using a wooden spoon, stir in enough egg white to form a soft piping consistency.

3 Put the mixture into a nylon piping bag fitted with a 2 cm/¾ inch plain piping nozzle (tip).

4 Pipe 20 rounds of mixture, well spaced, on to the lined baking sheets and press a split almond on each.

5 Place in a preheated oven at 170°C, 325°F, Gas Mark 3. Bake for 20–25 minutes or until lightly coloured and firm to the touch. Leave to cool on the baking sheets.

6 Cut around each macaroon to neaten the rice paper and dust with the icing (confectioners') sugar.

GINGER BISCUITS (COOKIES)

When spices first found their way into kitchens all over the world, they were much sought after by cooks who wished to add interest to their well-established recipes. Ginger was and still is a dominant spice.

MAKES 30

125 g/4 oz/½ cup butter

125 g/4 oz/⅔ cup soft light brown sugar

1 tbsp golden (light corn) syrup

1 tsp bicarbonate of soda (baking soda)

150 g/5 oz/1¼ cups plain (all-purpose) flour

1 tsp ground ginger

½ tsp ground mixed spice (apple pie spice)

1 Line 2 baking sheets with non-stick baking paper.

2 Put the butter, sugar and syrup into a large saucepan. Heat gently, stirring occasionally until melted. Remove from the heat and cool.

3 Stir in the bicarbonate of soda (baking soda) and allow to froth in the pan. Sift in the flour, ginger and mixed spice. Mix together with a wooden spoon and beat until evenly blended.

4 Place 24 walnut-sized balls of mixture, spaced well apart, on the baking sheets. Place in a preheated oven at 170°C, 325°F, Gas Mark 3 and bake for 10–15 minutes until golden brown. Cool on the baking sheet and remove with a palette knife when cold.

SHORTBREAD

Shortbread was once a traditional bridal cake, and was baked in hand-carved oak moulds before being cut into triangles.

SERVES 8

125 g/4 oz/1 cup plain (all-purpose) flour

60 g/2 oz/⅓ cup ground rice

60 g/2 oz/¼ cup caster sugar

125 g/4 oz/½ cup unsalted butter

caster (superfine) sugar for sprinkling

1 Mix together 1 tsp each of the flour and the sugar and use to dust an 18 cm/7 inch shortbread mould, if using. Line a baking sheet with greaseproof paper (baking parchment).

2 Sift the remaining flour and the ground rice into a mixing bowl. Add the remaining sugar. Cut the butter into pieces and rub into the flour mixture with your fingertips until the mixture begins to bind together. Knead into a soft dough.

3 Roll out on a floured work surface (counter) to the size of the mould, or into an 18 cm/ 7 inch round. Place the dough into the mould and press to fit neatly. Invert the mould on to the baking sheet and tap firmly to release the dough shape.

4 Bake in a preheated oven at 170°C, 325°F, Gas Mark 3 for 35–40 minutes until pale in colour. Sprinkle a little caster (superfine) sugar over the top and leave to cool on the baking sheet. Cut into wedges to serve.

TEA BISCUITS (COOKIES)

These centuries-old biscuits (cookies) were flavoured with caraway seeds and sometimes currants, but now they are often baked plain.

MAKES 40

150 g/5 oz/⅔ cup unsalted butter, softened

150 g/5 oz/⅔ cup caster (superfine) sugar

1 egg

¼ tsp vanilla flavouring (extract)

350 g/12 oz/3 cups plain (all-purpose) flour

1 tsp baking powder

1 tsp caraway seeds (optional)

60 g/2 oz/⅓ cup mixed dried fruit (optional)

caster (superfine) sugar for dusting

1 Beat the butter and sugar together with a wooden spoon until light and fluffy. Beat in the egg and vanilla flavouring (extract).

2 Sift in the flour and baking powder and mix to a soft dough. Add the caraway seeds and dried fruit, if using, to the dough. Knead until smooth and put in a plastic bag. Chill for about 1 hour.

3 Roll out the dough very thinly on a well-floured work surface (counter). Using a 6 cm/2½ inch fluted cutter, cut out about 40 biscuit shapes, re-kneading and re-rolling the trimmings if necessary. Arrange well apart on several baking sheets lined with greaseproof paper (baking parchment).

4 Place in a preheated oven at 180°C, 350°F, Gas Mark 4 and bake for about 15 minutes or until lightly coloured. Dust with caster (superfine) sugar if wished, and leave to cool on a wire rack.

ECCLES CAKES

These cakes originate from the town of Eccles in northern England. They were made with flaky pastry and filled with blackcurrants, sugar and mint leaves. Today's Eccles cakes are often filled with currants, sugar and butter.

MAKES 10

60 g/2 oz/¼ cup caster (superfine) sugar

1 tbsp cornflour (cornstarch)

1 tbsp chopped fresh mint

125 g/4 oz/1 cup blackcurrants

500 g/1 lb puff pastry

60 g/2 oz/¼ cup granulated sugar

1 Lightly flour 2 baking sheets.

2 Place the caster (superfine) sugar, cornflour (cornstarch) and mint in a bowl and stir until well mixed. Add the blackcurrants and mix well.

3 Cut the pastry in half and roll out thinly on a lightly floured work surface (counter). Using a 15 cm/6 inch plain cutter, or a saucer as a guide, cut out five rounds.

4 Place a spoonful of filling in the centre of each round using only half of the filling.

5 Brush the edges of the pastry with water and gather up the edges over the filling to form a pouch. Seal the edges together well. Turn the pouch over and roll lightly to a 9 cm/3½ inch round and place on the baking sheet. Repeat to make another five Eccles cakes.

6 Using a sharp knife, make three slits across the surface of each Eccles cake. Place in a preheated oven at 220°C, 425°F, Gas Mark 7 and bake for 15 minutes.

7 Dissolve the granulated sugar in 2 tbsp water, bring to the boil and boil for 1 minute. Remove the cakes from the oven, brush with sugar glaze and return to the oven for a further 5 minutes until golden brown.

TEA

Taking tea is a very popular pastime, and is made more enjoyable by the huge range of blends, flavours and strengths of tea that are now available from all over the world. This is a tried and tested method for making the perfect pot of tea.

SERVES 4

4 tsp fresh tea leaves

slices of lemon

fresh milk

---

1 Fill a kettle with fresh cold water and bring to the boil.

2 Just before the water boils, pour some of it into a good-quality china teapot to warm it.

3 Discard the water in the teapot and add 4 tsp of your chosen tea leaves (1 tsp per person) to the warmed pot.

4 As the water reaches a really good rolling boil, pour it into the teapot, allowing about 150 ml/¼ pint/⅔ cup water per spoonful of tea.

5 Allow the tea to infuse for 4–5 minutes to obtain a full flavour, but do not stir it.

6 Strain the tea into the cups, diluting it with boiling water if necessary.

7 Serve the tea with slices of lemon or cold milk. Opinion is divided as to whether to add milk to tea first or last. Tea was originally served with the milk (or cream) and sugar offered separately; later the milk was sometimes added first, followed by the tea. This was said to cook the milk partially, changing the

flavour of the tea. One rule,
however, has always remained
constant – the milk should
always be added cold.

INDEX